# SEXY LIKE A BOOK
## Book One
# Enchanting Voices

I0087219

# Sexy Like a Book
### Book One

# Enchanting Voices

## Edited by Patrice Juah

Lisa Harris 1st Place Winner
Victoria Daye 2nd Place Winner
Faith Gray 3rd Place Winner
Marshad Julia Beyslow - Finalist
Maxita Viola George - Finalist
Odell M. Garkpah - Finalist

VILLAGE TALES PUBLISHING | USA

A catalog record for this book is available from the
Library of Congress:
LCCN: 2017908158
ISBN: 9781945408175
eISBN: 9781945408182

Published By:
Village Tales Publishing
Lawrenceville, GA

Layout and Cover Design By:
OASS

www.villagetalespublishing.com
www.oass.villagetalespublishing.com

Printed in the United States of America

# Dedication

To all young girls across Liberia, who continue to dream and keep the flames of their dreams alive; in spite of all the challenges of living in Liberia today, this book is for you. We see you and celebrate you.

# Acknowledgements

We'd like to thank the Almighty God for endowing us with wisdom, courage and strength; without Him, none of this would have been possible.

Thanks to the Martha Juah Educational Foundation for birthing this vision and creating a platform to amplify the voices of Liberian girls.

Our gratitude goes out to Village Tales Publishing for believing in our vision and giving it wings. Thank you for holding our hands and journeying with us. We salute you!

A million thanks to the parents of our winners and finalists for their encouragement and support. Thank you for planting seeds of discipline and hardwork that will blossom in their hearts forever.

To the team at Cammepa Productions, we say thank you for standing with us and believing in this vision since day one.

Cummings Africa Foundation; thank you for providing transportation for our girls during our Books, Cupcakes & Conversations event.

Thanks to Forte Publishing for being one of the sponsors of our 1st Annual Sexy Like A Book Poetry Competition for Liberian Girls. The books you provided will inspire and enlighten the girls for years to come.

Our sincere appreciation goes to Vital Woman Magazine for partnering with us on their Mentor A Girl In Africa Project, which has provided books and mentors for our girls. We're forever grateful.

A very big 'thank you' to We-Care Foundation, for graciously giving us your space to use for our 1$^{st}$ Annual Books, Cupcakes & Conversations event.

Thanks to the judges of the Sexy Like A Book Poetry Competition for Liberian Girls, for helping us to identify and  select the most talented winners and finalists.

To the panelists and moderator of the "Conversations on Education" panel at our Books, Cupcakes & Conversations event, we say thank you for sharing your insights with us.

We want to thank the Daily Observer Newspaper for sharing our story.

Eden Summit team, thank you for your prayers, encouragement and support.

We also want to thank those who bought tickets and came out to support our Books, Cupcakes & Conversations event.

To everyone who has encouraged and prayed for us along this journey, we thank and appreciate you.

Thanks to all you readers and supporters for buying this book, and believing in the Sexy Like A Book vision, we extend a big gratitude hug to you. Thank you! Together we can say YES to books for girls!

"All along when people used the word "sexy", I thought it was only about being dressed half-naked. But now, I know that you can be sexy in so many ways, including being smart, true to yourself and believing in who you are."

— C. Samgie Peters, 17 years old, SDA High School, Paynesville, Liberia.

# Contents

# Foreword

Enchanting Voices echoes stories of a Liberia that could be, but struggles in the now. It echoes stories of hope and dreams; of courage and resilience; of possibilities and a future waiting to bloom.

This collection is a poetic celebration of youth, innocence, joy and emergence from a place of despair to one of progress and fulfilled dreams, if Liberians stay on the path of development, change their mindsets, and value Liberia for the true treasure that she is.

# Lisa Harris

First Place Winner

## Lisa Harris

 developed great interest in writing and reading, as she grew up in mostly quiet and well-grounded settlements that did not require much from her as a child, except her academic and best work. As a young girl, she has written several poems on various themes that are dear to her heart. She also wrote essays of all kinds throughout primary and secondary school.

 Lisa was born on October 29, 1994, in the capital of the Gambia, Banjul, and  grew up in Accra, Ghana, where she gained her pre-primary, primary, and one year of junior high school. She is truly a book lover and has strong principles that guide her in life. An adventurer who loves to visit new places, she loves to meet new people, and learn new things. She always tries to see the good in people and situations.

Currently, Lisa is a student at the University of Liberia, while she works with girls and young women in Liberia, aiding in their development in every capacity. The 2013 graduate of the Lott Carey Baptist Mission School is dedicated to improving the system of education, and the lives of young people, in Liberia.

## *Education, True Power of a Woman*

However you see it,
    and whatever you think of it,
Reading is the best,
    and it is powerful!

Yes! Education;
    a place of certainty,
and the key to success.

Young woman, you want to be successful?
    Get that diploma,
get that certificate, get that degree,
    get that honor, and walk with prestige
    through the journey of an educated life.

Oh education!
    What a precious and valuable tool.
The tool a young woman needs
    to kick out poverty, intimidation, and fear.

The tool that enables her
    To thrive through it all;
How beautiful is the mind
    of a young woman that reads.

A young woman that values books,
    and wouldn't trade them for anything;
How sexy she becomes,
    Like the books she reads.

Reading to learn,
    the one thing

that slaps ignorance in the face,
      Makes a woman the one in control.

When she says YES to education;
      she says YES to life, YES to power,
YES to wealth,
      and YES to the development of her nation.

I'm talking about education, young woman;
      One true gift
no one can take away from you.
      Get it, and it becomes yours forever;
Now that's what I call, beautiful
      and sexy just like a book!

## Poverty; Dream Killer

Poverty,
What a dream killer!
Oh Poverty!
I wish I could get you
Out of my life for good;
So I could fulfill my dreams
And reach my highest potential.

## Family

Family is a unit that is created and acknowledged by God, which makes it very important and unique. I usually come across the saying, "Family above everything" and "Nothing can be compared to family." Family members are the first people, friends, and acquaintances we build relationships with from birth. They give us a sense of belonging and make us feel needed and loved. Some family relationships are very constructive, trustworthy and dependable, while some are just the opposite. No matter what, family relationships are special; the connection and bond that exist between members are irreplaceable.

Over the years, I've studied the two types of family relations: consanguineous (relationship by blood) and conjugal (relationship by marriage). Besides these defined relationships, there are people we meet through life's many interactions, who at different intervals in our lives, can also be considered family, due to the mutual support and concern for each other's wellbeing. They make us feel special and are always willing to go the extra mile, just like real family members would.

LOVE, TOLERANCE, and SACRIFICE are some important components of blood/non-blood relationships. Love, as one of the most important ingredients of relationships, is a natural phenomenon that exists among family members; from parents to children, among siblings, between parents, or from father to children. Whether it is just a small family or an extended family, there are bonds that are formed and these bonds are based on love and our feelings towards members in the family. It is difficult to live together with others for a long period if we are not tolerant of one another. Tolerance does not exist only in family relationships alone, but in every other relationship there is. Family members have to be willing to accept the unacceptable at times, and they have to be willing to let go of the unforgivable in some situations, in order to maintain these relationships.

What is love without sacrifice? Once there is love in the family, there will always be sacrifice. Parents sacrifice for their children all the time; they deprive themselves of earthly possessions to give their children the best things in life. Education, for example, is a great sacrifice most parents make for their children. Once they know the importance and benefits of education, they go to the extreme to make sure their children get the best education they can get. Due to the bonds that are shared through blood, it is a natural responsibility that family members share with one another to ensure the support, growth, and development of another family member in good times, and during trying times.

Family relationships are never perfect. These relationships break up at some point and they sometimes seem impossible to mend. The amazing thing is, in the end, family relationships always find ways of being restored through reconciliation. Why? Because family will always be family, and like the saying goes: "blood is thicker than water."

I came across this and thought to share;


*'BoyfriEND', 'GirlfriEND', 'FriEND', 'BestfriEND', etc., last three letters are E.N.D., which means that someday they will all come to an end. But on the contrary, the last three letters in Family are, I.L.Y., which is interpreted as 'I LOVE YOU'.*


This signifies that no matter the trials and tribulations, differences and low-points family members face, the bond they share through blood and love will keep them together forever.

## A President With a Difference

Liberia, having had her fair share of chaos; instability, poverty, disease, amongst other calamities, needs more than an ordinary leader. With such devastation the country has faced in times past, mostly due to poor leadership and little or no vision, Liberia needs an extraordinary leader in order to rebuild and restore all that has been lost over the past years, and improve on successes and gains made. I strongly believe that Liberia needs a person who is God-fearing, patriotic, and compassionate to lead this country. Most Liberians lack true patriotism. One component of development is that the citizens of a country must have love for the country, and must be patriotic. To achieve this, patriotism has to be cultivated in the citizenry from the earliest stage of one's educational journey.

To put Liberia's growth and development into proper perspective, I've chosen to visualize myself as President of Liberia, and give a detailed breakdown of my plans and vision for the country. If I were the president of Liberia, I would ensure that education is priority number one. When a nation is educated, the livelihood and living conditions of its citizens are greatly improved. They contribute tremendously to the growth and infrastructural development of the nation. To prioritize education, I will increase the current education budget by 70% and set academic standards for teachers that are giving out knowledge and students that come in search of knowledge.

Furthermore, I will introduce policies that will ensure that primary schools are free. I will also create a student trust fund through which college and university students can access and obtain student loans to be paid over a specified period after obtaining their first degree. Practically, I would seek to build tuition-free vocational training centers across the country, especially in the rural areas. Young people can have access to knowledge in various technical studies and gain professional certificates and diplomas to facilitate career development, entrepreneurship, and self-employment.

Another area I would give priority focus is the agriculture sector. This sector has not been given the attention it deserves, thereby leading to our major staple food (rice) being imported into the country on a large scale. This leads to millions of dollars leaving our country that could have been used to create economic stability for the country, and jobs for our poverty-stricken mass population. Liberia has surplus of rich soil that can be productive. Investment in the soil is a lifetime achievement I would secure for Liberia and her future generations. I believe one of the major investments Liberia needs is to go back to the soil, and grow and produce what we eat.

In furtherance of my interest in agricultural activities, I would ensure that the Ministry of Agriculture creates a program where farmers across the country have access to finance to support their agricultural activities. In the rural areas, in particular, I would provide basic materials and equipment to help them develop and maintain their farms. This will facilitate the growth and production of food crops for their own consumption, and also for local trade, in order to earn a living and contribute to the economic vitality of the country.

Through partnerships with international organizations, and countries with success stories in the agriculture sector, I would support both subsistence and mechanized farming by providing access to finance to both small and large scale farmers, and plantations across the country, to enable them to grow and produce different kinds of food crops for the benefit of the country. This will subsequently contribute to a sharp increase in the employment rate by creating job opportunities. I will also ensure that personal income tax and business tax are decreased to a level that affords small, medium, and large businesses to grow. This will serve as an example that Liberians can live by, and become successful right here in Liberia.

Moreover, the cost and selling prices of these foods would be less, since they are now being produced in the country. Also, excess of the food crops produced can be exported to nearby countries, which would boost the economy of Liberia and help provide better standards of living for the people of Liberia.

With all these benefits and good results, the prioritization of agriculture and the efforts of the government through the Ministry of Agriculture, might yield, students at the university level will now be encouraged to study and further specialize in various fields of agriculture. This will enable them to emerge with new and sophisticated methods of farming to improve the farming system for years to come.

Another important initiative I would carry on as president is, youth empowerment. With the current youth population of Liberia estimated to be a little more than 65%, the young people have very important roles to play in the growth and development of Liberia. If they are neglected, the future of the country is also neglected. Therefore, I would seek to ensure that there are youth empowerment opportunities created in different sectors. These areas will enable the youth to meet their basic social needs, while gaining the requisite skills needed to take on important roles in their not-too-distant future.

Another relevant factor I would focus on as president is decentralization. Liberia has fifteen counties, but it seems as if it has just one, which is Montserrado

County, where the capital city, Monrovia, is located. Due to the problem of decentralization, development of other parts of the country has been difficult, thereby causing congestion and over-population. This is happening because all, or most, of the government ministries/agencies, private entities, factories, industries, etc., are located in Monrovia or around Montserrado County. Because of the economic activities and other benefits—better job opportunities, schools, residential communities, hospitals, and standards of living—compared to the rural areas, citizens tend to find no interest in other parts of the country besides Montserrado county, where these public and private agencies, institutions and corporations operate.

If I were the president of Liberia, I would build roads and bridges to connect towns and communities from one point to another. These roads and bridges would promote businesses and industrialization due to good infrastructure in those isolated and abandoned areas. This will also contribute to the creation of job opportunities and attract more people to move into those settlements.

Liberia has fourteen other counties and many beautiful cities in those counties apart from Montserrado County, and Monrovia City. Why isn't anyone paying attention to the other parts of the country? Do all the best things have to be in Monrovia? Does everyone have to work in Monrovia? Does everyone have to live in Monrovia City, or the best parts of Montserrado County? No, it doesn't have to be that way. We need more modernized hospitals, updated school buildings, profit-making companies, and industries built in other parts of the country. People living in those areas, who are unable to move to Monrovia, can have job opportunities, and the exposure to better standards of living as well. Development has to reach those places that aren't being thought of.

There are many different, and benefiting things I could do for Liberia and the people of Liberia if I were president. From investing in agriculture, promoting youth empowerment, revising the education system, decentralizing the country, to providing care and shelter homes for people living with disabilities, and the mentally challenged, amongst many other visions I have for this wonderful country.

Liberia is beautiful and promising. All she needs is a leader who will fall in love with, and care for her and her people. I have a vision for Liberia and Africa at large. I look forward to the time when I shall be opportuned to serve and realize that vision.

## Life in Liberia

Liberia is a small country, blessed with many dependable natural resources for the development and benefit of its people. Looking at the country, its people have faced, and been through, more adversities than some of them could possibly handle. Those would include the fourteen years of civil unrest, coupled with diseases, unstable economy, unemployment and extreme poverty. The many sad events that took place in the country over the past years have pushed the people of Liberia to become hard-hearted, and hateful towards one another; most of them living in frustration. Nonetheless, I strongly believe there is room for recovery, and Liberia is on the verge of rising up to a new dawn.

Life in Liberia can be described from different perspectives, but for the most part, living in Liberia is challenging and depressing. The country lacks those basic necessities that make life more suitable and bearable for its people. They lack good infrastructure and road networks that would enhance accessibility and modernization. The common people, comprising mostly of the young, old and disabled population, are the ones mostly affected by the harsh standard of living in the country.

The country is mostly populated with young people who have been coerced into various activities to seek success and realize their dreams. Many useful and beneficial opportunities are not being afforded the young people, to equip and enable them to become the future leaders they are expected to be. As a result, we find young people in Liberia not being exposed to the diversity of life, and unable to fully represent what they stand for and what society expects of them.

The Liberian society seems archaic and very difficult to live in. Young females are practicing cross-generational sex with older males their fathers' age for the sake of their survival; to obtain jobs, escape poverty, and the pressure to fit in. Young males have become homosexuals for the same reasons, with more young people becoming drug addicts. It is extremely unfortunate to see these acts unfolding in Liberia.

Looking at the elderly, what hope do they have? There's no one around to care for them and no policy in place to cater to their needs. What would they have to do then; go out on the streets to make ends meet? The old people of Liberia have seen, and been through way too much, but no one seems to care about them anymore. People have become selfish and self-centered that they care for no one else but themselves and their immediate families. Why won't they? Life in the country seems so uncertain; one minute you are at the peak and the next minute, you are at the bottom. Everyone is focusing on enriching themselves. Self-enrichment can be positive and rewarding, but it becomes negative due to the manner used by some Liberians to obtain it.

Considering the people living with disabilities, their survival in the country remains a mystery. They are challenged in so many ways, but it remains amazing how they push through from day to day. They have become the most marginalized group in Liberia and life for them is just difficult and unbearable. What some people in the country fail to realize is that disability is never chosen. It comes in an unexpected and unwelcomed manner, and in most situations, nothing can be done about it.

Sexual exploitation is on the rise every day. Young females are being taken advantage of on a daily basis; at the job sites, in schools, at their businesses, and the list goes on. And corruption has become the order of the day; a way of life for people living in Liberia. The sad truth about living in the Liberian society is that corruption does not only exist in the government, and amongst government officials, but it is clearly visible even among the common people. They tend to exploit their fellow Liberians at the least chance they get. This is unpatriotic, and only shows that Liberians do not love and care for one another as a people should. They definitely do not care about the growth and development of the country.

I have been trying to touch base, and talk, about several areas of deficiency in Liberia. The aspect of moral values is no exception. Generally, typical Liberian people (both young and old) seem to lack moral disciplines. They are not mindful of their words, and the use of profanity in public seems normal. I believe it is a result of improper upbringing of children in Liberia. In addition, it's the kind of environment they grow up in, climaxed by the Freedom of Speech policy allotted to the Liberian people.

Teenage pregnancy is another troubling factor in Liberia. Young females have become so exposed to social life that gets them involved in sexual activities at a tender age. Some of these girls lack mentorship and guidance from parents and successful older women, which results in their going astray and being victims of various conditions affecting girls and young women in Liberia. This is very troubling. We all should know by now that teenage pregnancy has many disadvantages and it does have its own effects on a society. Few girls have the courage to go back to school after they have become teenage mothers. What happens to the majority who never go back to school? In most cases, the children of these mothers never get the chance to know their fathers, which brings about single parenting. It's almost certain that these young mothers and their children tend to become a liability to society. When a woman is not educated to some level, the likelihood of her having her children educated is quite slim. This is where the poverty chain starts. Plus, we all know that an uneducated people in a society lead to a doomed society.

Education is another aspect I would like to emphasize on. Education is very important and its vitality to any society is incomparable. Liberia is still struggling in both aspects of providing and gaining quality and reliable education. The educational system in Liberia is very difficult. At the university level, there are limited choices of institutions, and very few areas of study to choose from, with little or no areas of specialization. There are barely qualified and effective instructors available to teach at the universities, which discourages students and makes them reluctant to go to school. Most qualified and educated people in Liberia did strive to gain international education through scholarships or sponsorship. I believe that more resources and priority have not been allocated to the education sector of Liberia, that is why these deficiencies exist. Liberians need quality education; education that they can depend on.

Discussing life in Liberia is an endless topic. I could go on and on, touching every sector; education, employment, health, business, policies, government, transportion, insecurity, justice, etc. They are all intertwined and nothing seems to work out the right way in the country. Life in Liberia is full of unrealized dreams and unachievable aspirations. One has to be very strong and determined in order to be successful. This is life in Liberia on a raw scale, and from the perspective of the majority.

Liberia is beautiful and its people are strong and resilient. Liberians have come a long way and I believe that they deserve more than what they are getting now. They need a better life. They need good hospitals and well trained doctors and nurses, so that they don't die from common diseases. They need quality education that they do not have to struggle for. They need every possible fundamental opportunity that they can get, in order to live fully and freely in their own country, and not have to travel to seek greener pastures in foreign lands. Let us not blame our present conditions on the long ended civil crisis. We may still be in the process of rebuilding, but Liberians are Liberia's problems. Until the people of Liberia recognize this, there is no moving forward for the country. There has to be renewed minds and patriotic people on fire for the country.

# Lisa Harris' Interview

Meet Lisa Harris, a 22-year-old sophomore at the University of Liberia.

**VTP:** Ms. Harris, where are you from?
**LH:** I am from Montserrado / Grand Bassa Counties, Liberia.

**VTP:** Tell us about your family.
**LH:** I come from a small family. I've lived with my parents and four siblings from my time of birth. My family traveled all over West Africa during the civil crisis in Liberia and then settled in Gambia, where I was born. We later moved to Ghana, where I grew up, and quite recently moved back home to Liberia. Life in Liberia has been a bit different for my family since we came back home. However, through it all, my parents have worked hard to provide the basic needs for my siblings and I to live well, and thrive for our own success.

**VTP:** What school do you attend?
**LH:** I attend the University of Liberia.

**VTP:** What do you enjoy most about school?
**LH:** I enjoy the fact that I get to meet and interact

with people from different cultures and backgrounds. These acquaintances, I believe, can develop lifelong relationships, which can be reliable and dependable in time to come.

**VTP:** What is your favorite subject? What do you like about it?
LH: At the university level, my favorite course is Social Science. I am interested in this course because it focuses on diversity, which I am attached to, and it includes various and different subject areas which help a person expand their horizon and learn about different aspects of the larger society.

**VTP:** What do you enjoy doing when out of school?
LH: When out of school, I enjoy working with children and youth in general; working along with girls and other young women.

**VTP:** Describe a typical day after school for you.
LH: A typical day after school for me is leaving the school's premises, after my last class and making my way to work at an after school program for kids; from grade levels 1 to 6 at 12th Street, Sinkor. I leave from work between 6 to 7 P.M. and make my way home.

**VTP:** Who is your most important source of inspiration?
LH: I don't have a person as my most important source of inspiration. I only have my dreams, which are the only things I can access whenever I need inspiration; and a sense of direction. My dreams are what inspire me and keep me going when times get tough.

**VTP:** Who or what would you like to become?

**LH:** I would like to become a humanitarian and a diplomat; representing Liberia at the international level. My love for diversity has prompted me to become an international person.

**VTP:** How would you inspire others?
**LH:** I would use my struggle and success story to inspire others. I would constantly share with others what it is taking me and what sacrifices I am currently making, along with how I have dealt with all the terrible things life may have thrown at me, to realize my dreams in time to come.

**VTP:** How would writing help you to achieve your dreams?
**LH:** Writing is something I love to do. It will contribute in the achievement of my dreams by serving as a source of inspiration for young people around the world.

**VTP:** What are your writing goals for the future?
**LH:** My writing goals for the future include being an author of inspirational writings, and inspiring girls and young women all over the world to not be afraid to dream; having a dream keeps us going and happy.

**VTP:** How do you want people to see you?
**LH:** I want people to see me as the young woman who sets herself apart from the rest of the crowd and always seeks to be different in her own way.

**VTP:** What seems challenging to you when it comes to writing?
**LH:** When it comes to writing, what seems challenging at times is keeping my mind fixed and concentrated on the specific topic of focus.

**VTP:** What do you like best about writing?

**LH:** Writing is beautiful; and for someone like me, what I like best about it is that it gives me the opportunity to explore my mind beyond my wildest dreams and expectations. It allows me to say the things I could not say verbally and allows me to freely express myself and live out my dreams in writing.

**VTP:** What do you like least about writing?

**LH:** What I like least about writing is the fact that it is time consuming, and it requires a concentrated and undisturbed mind.

**VTP:** What do you like to write about?

**LH:** I like to write, and I like to write on anything and everything I deem worthy of my time.

**VTP:** Do you have any advice for other writers?

**LH:** I would say to other writers that writing is a skill and if you have it, don't underestimate it; cultivate it and make time for it. You never know where it might take you.

**VTP:** What do you read outside of school?

**LH:** I basically read everything outside of school. The truth is I read more things outside of school than I read my own school work.

**VTP:** What is your favorite book? Why is it your favorite?

**LH:** My favorite book as of now is, "The Purpose Driven Life," written by Rick Warren. This book is my favorite because through His servant, God tells us the purpose for which He created us and what His expectations are of us. I love this book because in it, God tries to tell us that He is the reason for it all. It starts with Him and eventually, it will all end with Him.

**VTP:** Do you have any favorite authors?
**LH:** Yes! Rick Warren, the inspirational writer.

**VTP:** If you could be any character in a book, who would you be and why?
**LH:** If I could be any character in a book, I would be the victim of unfortunate circumstances. I would choose this character because I would practically want to show my readers how a victim of unfortunate circumstances can become a victor and rise to the top if he or she is determined and willing to be a survivor.

**VTP:** What hobbies do you have?
**LH:** My hobbies include reading, writing, and dreaming.

**VTP:** What do you enjoy most in your free time?
**LH:** In my free time, what I enjoy most is listening to music, blended with dreaming. These two take me to a beautiful world, revitalize my soul, and set it on fire to work hard to realize my full potential.

**VTP:** If you could go anywhere in the world, where would you go?
**LH:** I want to believe that this is a non-religious question. If it is, then I would go to the Caribbean, where there is beautiful ocean, beautiful people, and beautiful experiences. If the question is religious, I would go to Heaven, where I will find peace and rest and complete happiness.

**VTP:** Do you have anything specific that you want to say to your peers?

**LH:** Yes! I want to encourage my peers to explore many opportunities, work hard to achieve their goals and continue to dream. Do not be overwhelmed by the current situation. Never let the negatives get the best of you, and never be content until you see yourself in the place you have always dreamed of.

"I thought that being sexy meant getting dressed, looking at yourself and saying that you look good. Now I know that without education, skills and confidence, you're not sexy."

— Diamond C. Paygar, 14 years old;
Sr. Kathleen McGuire Memorial Catholic High School.

# Victoria Daye

Second Place Winner

## Victoria Daye

is a talented Liberian girl, who is twenty years of age. Born and raised in a Christian family, blessed with four siblings and lovely parents. She loves writing, singing, dancing and anything fun and creative. Victoria is charming, smart and outspoken. She is a former student of the Ricks Institute and was a Top 10 Honor Student in the class of 2015. She was also a winner of Black Girls Rock Leadership Camp USA/Liberia 2013, and attended Deeper Life Primary School in Gambia.

## The Perfect Lady

Imagine;
A world full of beauty and brains,
Respect for our intellectual ability,
Admired for our level of education.

Imagine;
A better world if we stayed focused
And break through the wall of ignorance.

Imagine;
The amount of change
We can make if we learn,
Discover new things and improve
Our ability to express ourselves
Through reading.

Imagine;
The impact of our voice
To those craving for a role model
Such distinct traits.

Imagine;
The opportunities,
Career paths and jobs awaiting us
If we dare to make the change.

Imagine;
Us standing for who we are,
What we are,
Our achievements.

Imagine;
Such change made by you.
Stop imagining;

It's time to make a difference,
Time to take over
And create our own "Knowledge Empire".

We are book sexy;
Sexy like a book.

## Poverty

As awful as your name sounds,
So are you, POVERTY!
A disgusting intruder,
Who brings sorrow,
Struggle and hardship.

With no heart of sympathy,
You cling like a hand bag,
Reducing one to half, or
Next to nothing, reflecting
Your negative nature on them.

No doubt,
You're a cursed descendant of the devil,
Cast out from the land of honey
And divine glory,
Looking for a host to feed on,
Just like the parasite you are.

## My Family, My Adorable Treasure

In a world so lost,
    I knew you.
In the struggles of life,
    I had you.
In blurred clouds of loneliness,
    you comforted me.
You've been my biggest strength in all-time,
    losing you is my fear.

Just like a seed buried under the soil,
    we grew together from one root,
 Watered with happiness,
    and baked by the blazing sun
    in times of sorrow.

We blossomed into beautiful flowers
    at the end of it all.
Strong in root
    and bond with love.

The only language we understand
    is care among ourselves.
When angry,
    we quarrel and nag,
but instantly renew it
    with love and forget our differences.

With no reward expected,
    we help each other,
gently wipe away our tears,
    grab each other
when we attempt to fall
    and stand again.

A love so genuine
        regardless of our flaws,
we seem to understand
        and view things differently,
from how the world may interpret
        our actions towards life,
and accept each other without questioning.

Our strength lies in all of us
        and our weaknesses
            reflect when we are separated,
but yet distance plays no role
        in our connection.
All I have and call mine
        is you, "MY FAMILY",
the backbone
        to who I am and what I have become.

## A Nation at Heart

Proud leader of my nation,
Yes, an inspiration for the future;
Bringing pride and victory is what I desire,
With determination to achieve it.

Restoring values to the youth of tomorrow,
Providing resources to students of our nation;
Equipping them to be strong enough
To face the outside world
Gives me more pleasure and zeal
For the reconstruction of a new nation.

Creation of employment,
And empowering our citizens,
Causing independent living
An aim that needs to be fulfilled.

Eradication of poverty,
And proper management
Of our own natural resources
Is a step ahead;
To enjoy our country's inheritance together.

A nation at heart
In the heart of a loving citizen,
Gives me no doubt of a different Liberia,
Craving to make a change,
And willing to make a change.

## Beauty of Liberty

"Soon morning day na break"
Life in Liberia, my Monrovia.
The duration of life is within
The 24-hours of a day,
The rest is in the hands of God.

Life in Liberia starts every morning
To the rising of the sun,
Welcoming a beautiful day
With another chance to start
All over again.

More hustle than you can ever imagine,
But yet, there's always a smile on our faces;
Forgetting the worries,
And making way out of no way.

People of one kind;
Amazing,
Unique,
Talented,
And beautiful.

The busy life of the people every morning,
Is a daily routine that inspires you to get up,
And look for what you aim to get.

Buyers and sellers,
Students and workers,
Noisy markets and traffic jam;
These crowds are on a busy errand,
And just enough alert,
You can get to start your journey.

Uptown,
Let's go Monrovia,
A place to be.
Reserved sites,
Nature's own beautiful treasures
Hidden within the heart of a country so loving.

LIBERIA,
Blessed with the perfect landscape and form;
Different people everywhere,
Making the best out of the hours,
Striving to achieve something.

As the sun gradually sets,
With few more hours to call it a day,
We cheerfully embrace the night,
Forgetting the tension of that day.

Jolly Jolly everywhere;
Dancing away our worries,
And appreciating life.

Making the last minutes worth it
With relaxation and rest,
While we await another day.

We believe
You only live once,
And every day is an opportunity.
L. I. B. life is beautiful.

# Victoria Daye's Interview

Meet 20-year-old, Victoria Daye, former Student of Ricks Institute.

**VTP:** Ms. Daye, where are you from?
**VD:** I'm from Grand Bassa County, Liberia.

**VTP:** Tell us about your family.
**VD:** I'm blessed with loving and caring parents and my five favorite crazy siblings. We always put God first and acknowledge Him in everything we do.

**VTP:** What school do you attend?
**VD:** I'm a former student of the Ricks Institute in Virginia, Liberia.

**VTP:** What do you enjoy most about school?
**VD:** I enjoyed the madness and fun that came along with school days, mainly from my batch.

**VTP:** What is your favorite subject? What do you like about it?
**VD:** My favorite subject is Biology and that's because it relates a lot to nature, our environment, and everything that links to us.

**VTP:** What do you enjoy doing when out of school?
**VD:** I enjoy helping Mom in her mini mart when out of school, that helps me to improve my marketing skills.

**VTP:** Describe a typical day after school for you.
**VD:** A typical day for me after school would be finding my way home and spending the rest of the day with my family.

**VTP:** Who is your most important source of inspiration?
**VD:** God is my most important source of inspiration.

**VTP:** Who or what would you like to become?
**VD:** I would like to be a well established and independent lady, who will give a helping hand to those who need it the most.

**VTP:** How would you inspire others?
**VD:** I will inspire others by motivating them. I believe this will boost their self-confidence and inspire them to do great things.

**VTP:** How would writing help you to achieve your dreams?
**VD:** Writing will serve as a form of platform to reach out and pass my message to those that need to hear it and be motivated.

**VTP:** What are your writing goals for the future?
**VD:** My writing goals for the future is to motivate, talk about God's love, and share my story with my readers.

**VTP:** How do you want people to see you?
**VD:** I would want people, young girls, to be precise, to

see me as a role model they can aspire to be, in order to make a unique difference in our society. With God's help, I'm working towards it.

**VTP:** What seems challenging to you when it comes to writing?
**VD:** The challenge I face when writing is when I'm limited to a particular theme, which I have to write on. I love writing what I'm moved to write about, and not what I'm told to write, but I still come up with my best after all.

**VTP:** What do you like best about writing?
**VD:** What I like best about writing is the playing on, and manipulation of words in your own way.

**VTP:** What do you like least about writing?
**VD:** What I like least is when I have to rewrite what I have written.

**VTP:** What do you like to write about?
**VD:** I like to write about love, nature, my creator (God), and life.

**VTP:** Do you have any advice for other writers?
**VD:** My advice to other writers is, words are magic, you have the ability to give life to what you write and make it possess what you want. Always do it to the best of your ability.

**VTP:** What do you read outside of school?
**VD:** Outside of school, I read novels and interesting online articles.

**VTP:** What is your favorite book? Why is it your favorite?

**VD:** My favourite book is the Bible, because it teaches me all that I should expect from humans, and how to relate to them. If you want to dig out all the devil's schemes and tricks, be sure to check it out. lol

**VTP:** Do you have any favorite authors?
**VD:** No, I don't have any favorite authors.

**VTP:** If you could be any character in a book, who would you be and why?
**VD:** I would be Cinderella because I will end up in the castle and live happily ever after. Awesome.

**VTP:** What hobbies do you have?
**VD:** My hobbies are singing, dancing, writing, acting (that's only in my room, lol), creative designing, talking, reading and chatting.

**VTP:** What do you enjoy most in your free time?
**VD:** I enjoy composing songs and writing poems during my free time.

**VTP:** If you could go anywhere in the world, where would you go?
**VD:** Touring the world, instead of a particular country, would be the perfect adventure.

**VTP:** Do you have anything specific that you want to say to your peers?
**VD:** To my peers I'd say, you're fearfully and wonderfully made. Chase your dreams and don't be scared of any obstacle that comes your way, it's only going to prepare you for something bigger ahead. Lastly, in a message from God, He said He loves you, and I do too.

# Faith Gray

Third Place Winner

*Faith Gray*

The daughter of Mrs. Henrietta Teta Gray & Dr. Mulbah Blamah Gray, Sr., Faith Gray was born on August 30, 1997. She is from Lofa County, and very proud of her Lorma heritage. She is a graduate of the Ricks Institute, in Virginia, Liberia. Her hobbies include designing, modeling, writing and reading interesting articles and books. What she hates most is being lied to, or being deceived.

Ms. Patrice Juah is her role model. Her favorite color is sky blue, and she loves being around children. Faith's goal is to become a Medical Doctor, and one of Liberia's best female writers.

Her favorite quotation is, "It is not how many times one falls, but how many times one falls and can still get up and move again".

## The Stranger That Changes Everything

With a piece of lappa tied around her,
Shy and scared,
Carefully avoiding her common experiences,
From the stream of a four-hour walk from home,
Where only her kind
Is found cleaning his wearing;

Back to where she is,
With no option but to accept this as home,
Again, into smoke
That runs tears down her cheeks,
Preparing meals again,
Because she is "she";

Where the home is heaven for some,
And torment for others;
Washing, cooking, cleaning,
And waiting to be told nothing was done,
A thing for "she".

Discussions for the benefit of the whole town,
But she is not allowed to be there,
Because of "she".

But her encounter with you,
Changed everything; EDUCATION.
You made her discover her true self;
Yes, she can be whatever she wants to be,
Anything!

Bold, confident,
Self-dependent,
Breaking gender barriers,
Empowered to speak, write,

And defend her family and herself.

Truly,
Those of her kind that know you,
Never get disappointed.
You are always there, anytime,
Every time.

She now lives happily,
And confidently faces the future.
Being very close to the security of your gate;
Through reading, she goes places
She could have never been.

Her rights and responsibilities
Are revealed to her because of you.
You make her so important,
That her impact in the lives of many,
At home and abroad, is beyond expression.

She waits on you
As the moon awaits the sun.
Because of you,
She knows her security.
Reading, who in turn
Makes her know more of you.

You develop her mind,
Aid her discovery of potential,
And Boost her imagination and creativity.

She finds vital skills for jobs in you,
She can't seem to get you off her mind.

Inspiration of life,
The mother of intellect and beauty,

Swims in her brain,
Inspiring, motivational,
Eloquent, knowledgeable, attractive;
All because she became sexy like a book.

## *Poverty, the Reckless Force*

Poverty,
>> the hard-times of my life;
>> You made me grieve
>>> and disappointed,

Disappointed,
>> like a hungry dog;
>> Because of you,
>>> I cannot do anything on my own.

Poverty,
>> you are a disgrace to my home.
>> I can never be happy with you in my life.

Poverty,
>> the reckless force.

## My Guardian Angel

There is no one in this world
That can compare to you.
You are like a root that holds a tree,
Without you, how will I stand?

You support me in everything I do.
Your warm and comfortable arms embrace me.
You are my guide,
Who shows me the way.

Your warm and cool arms you give me,
When I need you most,
You are my hero
That rescues me in times of trouble.

My guardian angel,
Who watches out for me.
You love and care about me,
Even when I hurt you most.

Oh, how sweet you are,
My guardian angel.
You provided my needs,
And made me who I am today.

Because of you,
I am now proud;
Educated,
Intelligent,
Brilliant,
And sexy like a book.

## Sweet With Money

Her land is filled with beautiful sites,
    Blessed with resources,
And cherished by many.
    The aroma
Of her delicious palm butter she prepares,
    Can only be eaten by few,
And for others,
    It's just smell, no taste.

Her home is heaven for some,
    And misery for others.
Her beauty is so astonishing,
    You take solace in her presence.
Everything about her is sweet with money,
    Only a few might enjoy her sweetness
And for others,
    It's just, "mmmmh, aaaay na easy ooh,"

Because she is sweet only with money.

## Hoping for Opportunity

I wish I could have an opportunity
    To become a leader,
An opportunity when I shall change Liberia;
    From poverty to prosperity,
    From the poorest to the richest,
    From a village to a country.

An opportunity;
    When I shall hear the voices of the hungry,
When I shall listen to the voices of the abused,
    Abandoned and frustrated.

An opportunity;
    When I shall care and listen to my citizens,
    Empower and improve
    The messy educational system,
    To a better educational system.

An opportunity;
    When I shall stand up
And govern my people with patriotic power,
    An opportunity as such,
    Is what I search for.

# Faith Gray's Interview

Meet 19-year-old graduate of Ricks Institute, Faith Gray.

**VTP:** Where are you from, Faith?
**FG:** Although I was born in Montserrado, I am originally from Lofa County, Liberia.

**VTP:** Tell us about your family.
**FG:** Well, my family is a big family. I have 12 siblings; seven brothers and five sisters. I am the last child of my parents. We love and help each other as our father has taught us to be.

**VTP:** What school do you attend?
**FG:** I'm a recent graduate of the Ricks Institute, located in Montserrado County, Liberia.

**VTP:** What do you enjoy most about school?
**FG:** Wow! What I enjoyed most about school was the fun we had while learning.

**VTP:** What is your favorite subject? What do you like about it?
**FG:** My favorite subject is Biology, and what I like about it is that it makes me to discover new things about my body and my environment.

**VTP:** What do you enjoy doing when out of school?
**FG:** When out of school, I enjoyed having essential conversations with my friends, or just having a relaxing time at a cool place.

**VTP:** Describe a typical day after school for you.
**FG:** On a typical day when I was in high school, I sometimes attended extra classes until 4:00 PM, or went to work at my school's 4-H Garden; and then by 5:00, I'd go home, eat, and rest for my studies at night.

**VTP:** Who is your most important source of inspiration?
**FG:** My most important source of inspiration is my lovely mom.

**VTP:** Who or what would you like to become?
**FG:** I would like to become a medical doctor or a cardiologist, and at the same time, an enterpreneur in agriculture, an inspirational writer and a fashion designer.

**VTP:** How would you inspire others?
**FG:** I can inspire others by achieving my goals and becoming a positive role model.

**VTP:** How would writing help you to achieve your dreams?
**FG:** Writing will help me to achieve my goals in that when I write, I write about things that are affecting my home, environment, country, and my world; and this motivates me to have more passion for what I want to do.

**VTP:** What are your writing goals for the future?

**FG:** I'd like to become one of Liberia's best motivational writers, and a poet.

**VTP:** How do you want people to see you?
**FG:** I want people to see me as an intelligent, eloquent, and productive young woman, and a positive role model for others.

**VTP:** What seems challenging to you when it comes to writing?
**FG:** What is challenging for me when it comes to writing is the reluctance with which I sometimes approach the process. That makes it difficult for me to write.

**VTP:** What do you like best about writing?
**FG:** What I like most about writing is that it helps me to express myself freely through words, and also broadens my mind.

**VTP:** What do you like least about writing?
**FG:** What I like least about writing is, it can be time consuming.

**VTP:** What do you like to write about?
**FG:** I like to write about things that are happening around me; or to me, my family and my friends.

**VTP:** Do you have any advice for other writers?
**FG:** My advice to other writers is to be creative in their writing, and they should express themselves with passion.

**VTP:** What do you read outside of school?
**FG:** When out of school, I sometimes read newspapers, books or magazines.

**VTP:** What is your favorite book? Why is it your favorite?
**FG:** My favorite book is called, "Questions That Young People Ask, Answers That Work." I like it because it educates me on moral standards, and about things God wants us to do, especially the youth. He does want us to live morally upright lives as His chosen generation.

**VTP:** Do you have any favorite authors?
**FG:** No, I don't have any favorite authors.

**VTP:** If you could be any character in a book, who would you be and why?
**FG:** If I am a character in a story, I'd like to be a character that will suffer and then later starts to enjoy, because I want people to know that success comes with pain and struggle. I'd also want others to know that they can overcome their challenges, no matter what.

**VTP:** What hobbies do you have?
**FG:** My hobbies are, modeling, singing, reading and writing.

**VTP:** What do you enjoy most in your free time?
**FG:** In my free time, I enjoy relaxing and having good conversations.

**VTP:** If you could go anywhere in the world, where would you go?
**FG:** If I could go anywhere in the world, I'd go to Spain.

**VTP:** Do you have anything specific that you want to say to your peers?

**FG:** What I want to say to my peers is that you should always be positive, dream big, and work towards your goals. Also, make use of every opportunity you have. Know that you are more than a conqueror.

# Marshad Beyslow

Finalist

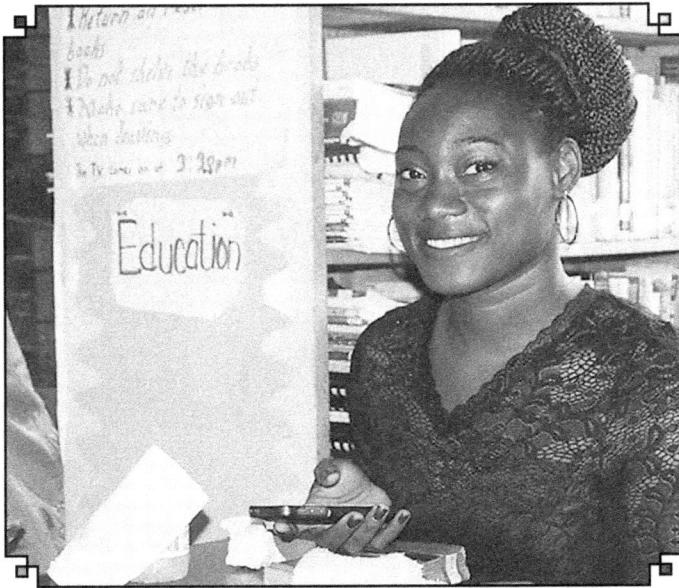

## Marshad Julia Beyslow

is the first of three children of Mr. Shadrick Beyslow and Mrs. Margaret Beyslow. Her other two siblings are Shirley S. Beyslow and Abdallah E. Beyslow.

Marshad was born on February 7, 2000, at the Ricks Community Clinic in Lower Virginia, Montserrado County, Republic of Liberia. She is 17-years old. She graduated from Ricks Institute with the class of 2015/2016, and is currently enrolled at Stella Maris Polytechnic.

Marshad likes reading, writing, public speaking, and making new friends with good morals and integrity; envisioning how she wants to be when she grows up. One of her favorite quotes is from one of Mr. Ben Carson's books titled, "Think Big" and "You have a brain use it".

## Who Am I ?

I'm Sexy;
You see me,
You feel me,
You never knew you'd need me.

What makes me,
Is complexed.
What makes me,
Is mind boggling.

I'm a combination
Of three joined together
On a rocking speed.

I'm intelligent,
I'm beautiful,
I'm confident;
Three.

Who can match me?
Who can match all that I am?
I woke up from deep, deep, slumber,
I grew up from under a man's thumb.

My eyes are open,
Wide awake,
I know what I want;
And I go for it.

Give me the worst,
And I'll make the best of it.
That's what makes me, me;
A woman.

## Daddy's Little Girl

You'll always be little to Daddy,
You'll always be his little girl ;
You bring smiles to his face,
And laughter to his life.
He'll walk to the ends of the earth,
And back to see you safe.

Oh, how when you think you've grown,
Then Daddy says,
You have not reached your full moon.
He'll fight off boys with machetes,
And threaten a lot of men.
But with tears in his eyes,
He'll give you away
To that one special person.

He will tell him,
You have my precious little one,
She'll always be my little girl.
Whose diapers I changed,
I saw her first walk,
Watched her first tooth grow,
And heard her first word;
I pushed her on a swing,
And cleaned her skinned knee.

My heart rests a bit,
To see this enchanting smile on her face.
Take care, my girl,
You'll always be Daddy's little one.

## *Notes on Poverty*

Tears mixed with dirt
    streak down my face,
      My bones,
          they protrude out of my body;
          The poor child I am,
            yearns for relief.

## My Kind of President

President! President!
When I am President,
What is to be done,
Is my question.
How will it be done,
Is my question.
Will you join me,
Is your question.

With hands held together,
We'll build my Liberia;
I'll build bridges over rivers,
I'll put roads through mountains,
I'll build schools in interiors,
I'll eradicate poverty from my Liberia.

President! President!
Only the wailing of my sirens,
I long to hear.
The wailing of ambulance sirens
Disturbs me,
So, good and affordable
Healthcare I'll provide.

I'll make my country clean,
I'll light up my country like the night sky,
I'll enhance its natural beauties;
The beaches,
The rivers,
I'll lift my people from the dust.

And then,
I'll showcase

My Liberia to the world,
Lone Star,
Shining brightly to all.

## The Liberian Life

Just like every other African place,
The sun shines deeply in my face,
Sand grains my foot sinks into,
And they caress my toes.

The blue waters I see,
The hills gently slope,
The trees and forest going green,
I sit, I watch and listen.
The natural air
Makes me take in a deep breath;
Life in Liberia this is.

I wake up,
I sell,
I go to bed hungry.
The hustle is hard,
Too many sellers,
Not enough buyers.

Yana[1] boys carrying their wares
Up and down Broad Street.
The hustle, the bustle, is real.
Life in Liberia, this is.

My kind of Liberia
Is rosy, not always.
It's hard, not all the time,
It's full of ups and downs.

The problems
Do not make me run,
They build me up

1    *peddlers who offer merchandise for sale along the streets.*

For stronger challenges.
With all the good and the bad,
I'll stay nowhere else;
The life in Liberia, this is.

# Marshad Julia Beyslow's Interview

Meet Marshad Beyslow, a 17-year-old freshman at Stella Maris Polytechnic.

**VTP:** Where are you from?
**MJB:** I'm from Montserrado County, Liberia

**VTP:** Tell us about your family.
**MJB:** My family is a small family that consists of my parents and my two siblings. We are a God-fearing family that believes that the family that prays together stays together.

**VTP:** What school do you attend?
**MJB:** I attend the Stella Maris Polytechnic.

**VTP:** What do you enjoy most about school?
**MJB:** I enjoy the challenge of learning new things .

**VTP:** What do you do when out of school?
**MJB:** I enjoy reading, writing and making jokes with my friends.

**VTP:** Describe a typical day after school for you.
**MJB:** On a typical day after school, it is already late evening and there's not much to do, but I help my little brother with his schoolwork, and do my own

schoolwork.

**VTP:** Who is your most important source of inspiration?
**MJB:** I am my most important source of inspiration.

**VTP:** Who or what would you like to become?
**MJB:** I would like to be a lawyer, diplomat and a writer.

**VTP:** How would you inspire others?
**MJB:** I would inspire others through my writing and careers.

**VTP:** How would writing help you to achieve your dreams?
**MJB:** Writing would help me to achieve my dreams because through writing, I read, analyze and I learn faster; writing puts me way ahead of my peers.

**VTP:** What are your writing goals for the future?
**MJB:** I want to be a world renowned author.

**VTP:** How do you want people to see you?
**MJB:** I want people to see a girl who's coming up in a world of gender equality and is determined to be on top.

**VTP:** What seems challenging to you when it comes to writing?
**MJB:** The challenging part of writing is being given a topic to write on.

**VTP:** What do you like best about writing?
**MJB:** Writing is an outlet for me, it helps me to let go of my frustrations and keeps me sane.

**VTP:** What do you like least about writing?
**MJB:** The way I write in bits and pieces and always have to have a piece of paper, because creativity can strike at any time.

**VTP:** What do you like to write about?
**MJB:** Anything and everything.

**VTP:** Do you have any advice for other writers?
**MJB:** You can write anything and everything. Keep your mind open and and you'll find a lot of things to inspire you.

**VTP:** What do you read outside of school?
**MJB:** I read novels.

**VTP:** What is your favorite book? Why is it your favorite?
**MJB:** My favorite book is DADDY, by Danielle Steele. I like it because it was the first novel I read and liked, that got me interested in reading voraciously.

**VTP:** Do you have any favorite authors?
**MJB:** Yes. My favorite authors are, Danielle Steele, John Grisham, and Mary Higgins Clark.

**VTP:** If you could be any character in a book, who would you be and why?
**MJB:** I would be Jane, a character in a book written by Danielle Steele called, BIG GIRL. She had issues with self confidence because of her body image, and the parents she had. BIG GIRL is a journey with Jane as she struggles to overcome her challenges and come out feeling a lot more positive about herself.

**VTP:** What hobbies do you have?

**MJB:** Reading.

**VTP:** What do you enjoy most in your free time?
**MJB:** I enjoy reading mostly in my free time.

**VTP:** If you could go anywhere in the world, where would you go?
**MJB:** I would go to Paris, France.

**VTP:** Do you have anything specific that you want to say to your peers?
**MJB:** I would tell my peers that education is the key to success, as quoted. With God in one hand and education in the other hand, you can be a success in whatever you do.

# Maxita George

Finalist

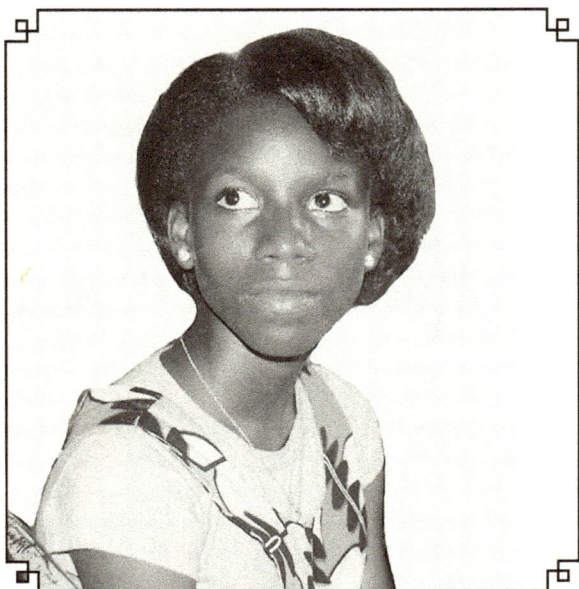

## *Maxita Viola George*

is an eighth grade student of Ricks Institute; blessed to the union of Mr. and Mrs. Maxwell S. George. The last of four siblings, she was born on April 7, 2004.

A devout Christian, Maxita is the current CHILD OF THE YEAR, 2016/2017 at Providence Baptist Church. Her hobbies include reading, interacting with friends, and dancing. She lives with her family in the Moulton Corner Community in Brewerville, Montserrado County.

## Glittering Creatures Won't Be Hidden

From their struggles,
A lot of them show bruises.
When leaders are questioned,
They give excuses.
It hurts when they suffer from abuses,
Today, I can hear different voices.

When I see heroines,
From my mind fades their losses;
Their strength claims their rights
And gives justice to the masses.

Over are the days
Of weeping and sad faces;
Be strong and make a change,
Awesome like true-love kisses.
The beauty of your mind
Speaks loud in different places.

In you I see greatness,
Let the love for ink
Print glow in your sexiness.
Keep roaring like a lioness,
Don't allow them to mistake
For stupidity your kindness.

Shine in all darkness,
Show others your way
Through your brightness.
Rape, violence, and segregation
Are wickedness.

I have long seen you
Pay back with kindness,

That's why I love your gentleness;
Because your patience
Overcomes men's madness.

## *Poverty Around Us*

Communities suffer for money
    And strive each day,
Children beg and pray for grace
    To go to school
And live day by day;

Begging has forced its way
    Into social life,
I pray for a better life
    In Liberia today.

## An Ode to Family

Being the smallest in the Family
        Is a gift from God.
My life is not always perfect,
        But always beautiful;
I am proud of who I am
        And I think God loves me
        Just the way I am.

Little Girl,
        Oh, so small,
One day
        I will be big and tall.
My family watched me
        While I laughed and played,
        Their love for me grows every day.

Sometimes life is a struggle,
        But my dear sweet family
Is always there to comfort me.
        As the smallest in my family,
I am like a bird in the nest
        Waiting to be loved,
        Cared for and protected by my family.

To my dear family,
        I will forever be the smallest.

## A Different Kind of President

If I were the President of Liberia,
I would always speak the truth,
And prosecute any form of corruption.

Ensure that there will be
More than enough jobs for everybody,
I would invest in infrastructure.

Not just roads and bridges,
But schools, playgrounds,
Parks, community centers,
Clinics and libraries.

Aim to support Girls' empowerment,
I will lower the cost of education.
I feel everyone deserves to learn
And get a proper education.

I will help the poor
And homeless everywhere.
I would focus entirely
On achieving what I think most Liberians want;
A stable and productive economy.

## Lens on Liberia

In Liberia,
>For a common man,
>>Life is not easy.

There are less job vacancies
>And more jobs that are not good.
>>The education system is very poor.
>>>We have no good health facilities.

In Liberia,
>Women and girls
>>Who can't get proper education
>>>Sometimes see themselves ending up
>>>>As prostitutes or market women.

Being a market woman is not bad
>As being a prostitute,
>>But I believe
>>>They both have challenges.

From my point of view,
>Life in Liberia is not easy,
>>Because we cannot always have the best,
>>>But God has continuously blessed
>>>>This great nation.

# Maxita Viola George's Interview

Meet 13-year-old Maxita Viola George, 8th grader at Ricks Institute.

**VTP:** Where are you from?
**MVG:** I'm from Bomi County, Liberia.

**VTP:** Tell us about your family.
**MVG:** My family is very lovely. My parents are alive, and I have three siblings; a sister and two brothers.

**VTP:** What school do you attend?
**MVG:** I attend the Ricks Institute.

**VTP:** What do you enjoy most about school?
**MVG:** I mostly enjoy the extracurricular activities.

**VTP:** What is your favorite subject? What do you like about it?
**MVG:** My favorite subject is Science, because it helps me to know a lot of things about my future career – Gynecology.

**VTP:** What do you enjoy doing when out of school?
**MVG:** I enjoy finding solutions to problems, meeting new people and hearing about their experiences.

**VTP:** Describe a typical day after school for you.
**MVG:** I mingle with friends and try to learn new football tricks from my brother. I participate in household chores and help make dinner.

**VTP:** Who is your most important source of inspiration?
**MVG:** My inspiration comes from beautiful young women who are influential.

**VTP:** Who or what would you like to become?
**MVG:** I would like to become Africa's best Gynecologist.

**VTP:** How would you inspire others?
**MVG:** I would inspire others by doing my job the best way I can, and by helping others uncover their hidden potentials.

**VTP:** How would your writing help you to achieve your dreams?
**MVG:** By sharing my experiences and inspiring others to dream big.

**VTP:** What are your writing goals for the future?
**MVG:** I want to write great leadership and inspirational books.

**VTP:** How do you want people to see you?
**MVG:** I want people to see me as a great leader and a heroine in the society.

**VTP:** What seems challenging to you when it comes to writing?
**MVG:** That you sometimes think your thoughts and

ideas aren't good enough.

**VTP:** What do you like best about writing?
**MVG:** What you think makes no sense will always make sense to someone else.

**VTP:** What do you like least about writing?
**MVG:** I do not appreciate when people criticize my best, but do not suggest how I can improve.

**VTP:** What do you like to write about?
**MVG:** I like to write about issues that bother girls.

**VTP:** Do you have any advice for other writers?
**MVG:** Do what you do, and do it to the best of your ability.

**VTP:** What do you read outside of school?
**MVG:** I read children's books, and learn new things about children's needs, because I feel the urge to support those who are helpless and defenseless out there.

**VTP:** What is your favorite book? Why is it your favorite?
**MVG:** 'The Gods are not to blame" is my favorite book. It has lots of debatable issues, and it teaches incredible lessons to new and upcoming storytellers/ writers.

**VTP:** Do you have any favorite authors?
**MVG:** My favorite author is Ola Rotimi.

**VTP:** If you could be any character in a book, who would you be and why?
**MVG:** I would love to be a leader of a group because I have a passion for leadership, and I like to demon-

strate the values and principles of my life for others to follow as a good example.

**VTP:** What hobbies do you have?
**MVG:** I like to read, write songs, stories and news. I also love to dance and have fun with friends.

**VTP:** What do you enjoy most in your free time?
**MVG:** Listening to music, reading books, dancing and talking with friends.

**VTP:** If you could go anywhere in the world, where would you go?
**MVG:** If I were to go anywhere in the world, that place would be Dubai.

**VTP:** Do you have anything specific that you want to say to your peers?
**MVG:** We all should unite to develop our beloved country. In doing so, we should not be deterred by what others may say. Instead, we should be focused, have faith and trust in God.

# Odell Garkpah

Finalist

## *Odell M. Garkpah*

is seventeen years old, and in the 11ᵗʰ grade at the Christian Martyrs Academy. She lives with her family in Marshall, Margibi County, although she hails from Grand Bassa County. Odell loves to read, watch movies and cook. One day, Odell aspires to become a nurse, and a fashion designer.

# Reflections on Poverty

In my view,
When it comes to poverty,
Especially in some areas,
Some people experience poverty
Throughout their lives.

Some experience it in many ways,
Including: No money
To pay their children's school fees,
No food to eat,
Or means to meet their daily needs.

So many say,
Their life is helpless,
Worthless and useless;
All because of poverty.

## Plight of an African Girl

Born in a small hut,
    Life itself was destined
        To be a heavy load.

A load I'd carry till eternity,
    And accept all the things
        Which were asked of me
           By my parents and society.

I was denied the right to an education,
    And told that my ultimate dream
        Was to become someone's wife.

They said that
    I would amount to nothing in life.
        To them, my life is like an egg
        Which can crack at anytime.

And once it cracks,
    It would shatter into pieces.
        They said that doing house work
        Would be my occupation,
        And marriage and children,
        My big property and final destination.

Those words pierced at my heart
    And collided in my ears.
        I was at a crossroads;
        Do I accept my fate and give up?
        Or, do I stay strong and keep pushing?

In that moment,
    I heard a tiny voice whisper,
        "Don't get tired.

In order to achieve your goals,
You have to struggle more."

So I braced myself and stood tall
And today I'm here,
Enlightened, equipped,
And on this journey
With an education for life.

## *My Special Family*

My family,
My special family;
A great gem which blesses
And uplifts its members.

A source of strength
And inspiration;
A foundation of knowledge
And motivation.

I love my family,
And they love me too.
I want to make them proud,
As they make me proud every day.

We're unique,
But aren't perfect,
We're strong in our differences,
And perfectly held together;

Like a beautiful family portrait.

## L.I.B. Seesaw Life

Life in Liberia is like a seesaw;
A mix of ups and downs,
Progress and challenges,
Poverty and riches,
Sunshine and rainfall,
Sorrow and happiness.

With unity and conviction,
We can stand together as one people,
We can develop and improve our land;
Promote and support all its sectors
For lasting growth and development.

We can enhance the works of Liberians,
And showcase our best to the world.

## Heart of a President

A president,
That thinks development for the country,
A president,
That cares for the poor and needy,
A president,
That prioritizes education for all,
A president,
That inspires and encourages children to learn.

If I become president of Liberia,
I will build and strengthen our health facilities;
Maximizing the resources of the land
To create opportunities for a better future.
In short,
I'd be the people's president;
A president with a caring heart.

# Odell M. Garkpah's Interview

Meet 17-year-old, Odell M. Garkpah

**VTP:** Where are you from?
**OMG:** I'm from Grand Bassa County, Liberia.

**VTP:** Tell us about your family.
**OMG:** I'm from a big and loving family; the only child of my mother and the 15$^{th}$ grandchild of my grandmother.

**VTP:** What school do you attend?
**OMG:** I attend the Christian Martyrs Academy.

**VTP:** What do you enjoy most about school?
**OMG:** I enjoy how our lessons are presented. The teachers are well trained and the learning facility is conducive.

**VTP:** What is your favorite subject? What do you like about it?
**OMG:** My favorite subjects are Economics and Accounting. They are my favorite subjects because they help me to learn how to solve problems and to think critically.

**VTP:** What do you enjoy doing when out of school?
**OMG:** I enjoy reading magazines and books.

**VTP:** Describe a typical day after school for you.
**OMG:** After school, I go home, do my assignments, help with household chores, study and keep company with my grandma.

**VTP:** Who is your most important source of inspiration?
**OMG:** My late father was a great source of inspiration for me, but now that he's no more, my grandma is my biggest inspiration. She counsels me when I'm going down the wrong path, and encourages me with her life's stories and experiences.

**VTP:** Who or what would you like to become?
**OMG:** I would like to become a fashion designer. I'm also inspired by movie stars and would like to do some acting one day.

**VTP:** How would you inspire others?
**OMG:** I want to encourage and motivate young people to build up their foundation in education, in order to achieve their goals and dreams, and to help in the development of Liberia.

**VTP:** How would writing help you to achieve your dreams?
**OMG:** I feel like writing will help me to improve my confidence, writing skills and reading ability. It will also help me to express myself better.

**VTP:** What are your writing goals for the future?
**OMG:** I will continue to write, work on improving my

writing skills and combine it with fashion design and my other passions.

**VTP:** How do you want people to see you?
**OMG:** I want people to see me as a help to the nation, a renowned fashion designer and writer.

**VTP:** What seems challenging to you when it comes to writing?
**OMG:** The most challenging thing with writing is how some small words can be difficult to spell.

**VTP:** What do you like best about writing?
**OMG:** What I like best about writing is that it gives me the opportunity to express myself and tell others about my experiences and story.

**VTP:** What do you like least about writing?
**OMG:** Sometimes it requires a lot of concentration and it can seem like too much work.

**VTP:** What do you like to write about?
**OMG:** Myself and my life's story.

**VTP:** Do you have any advice for other writers?
**OMG:** Be encouraged and continue to write. And if it doesn't make sense, it will make sense to others, continue to write and express yourself no matter how difficult it may seem.

**VTP:** What do you read outside of school?
**OMG:** I read books, magazines, and articles about pop culture and celebrities.

**VTP:** What is your favorite book?
**OMG:** The Twelfth Night by William Shakespeare.

**VTP:** Why is it your favorite?
**OMG:** It teaches one how to reconcile with one's enemy and live at peace. The book is about loving yourself, your friends and family.

**VTP:** Do you have any favorite authors?
**OMG:** Although he's widely known as an actor, Will Smith is my favorite author.

**VTP:** If you could be any character in a book, who would you be and why?
**OMG:** I'd be Cinderella because she was submissive and courageous in pursuit of her dreams.

**VTP:** What hobbies do you have?
**OMG:** I love to read books and magazines, and I enjoy singing, and watching movies.

**VTP:** What do you enjoy most in your free time?
**OMG:** During my free time, I enjoy listening to music.

**VTP:** If you could go anywhere in the world, where would you go?
**OMG:** I'd go to Australia.

**VTP:** Do you have anything specific that you want to say to your peers?
**OMG:** Young people should stay focused on their education and put in effort. Success demands education. They should also look for good mentors.

"I want to encourage and motivate young people to build up their foundation in education, in order to achieve their goals and dreams, and to help in the development of Liberia."

~ Odell M. Garkpah, Finalist, Sexy Like A Book Poetry Competition for Liberian Girls.

# About *Sexy Like A Book*

Launched in 2015, Sexy Like A Book is a Martha Juah Educational Foundation initiative, designed to inspire young women and girls to improve their perspective on reading, literacy and education.

With 61 million girls out of school globally, the need to create educational programs, opportunities, and spaces that engage and support girls along their educational journey is more critical now than ever.

Sexy Like A Book helps in combating the high rate of illiteracy in Liberia, by cultivating a culture of reading that transcends the classrooms, and motivates girls to be intelligent, poised, creative and assertive visionaries, who contribute to their communities and the world.

Since its founding, we've gone on to launch the Annual Sexy Like A Book Poetry Competition for Liberian Girls, to encourage young girls to write and tell their stories their way. The winners and finalists of the competition receive mentorship, publication in our annual Sexy Like A Book anthology, and are awarded academic prizes. They will each serve as contributors to the writing column of our newly launched Sexy Like A Book website.

We've published Sexy Like A Book, Book One - Enchanting Voices, an anthology of poems written by the winners and finalists of the 1st Annual Sexy Like A Book Poetry Competition for Liberian Girls, courtesy of Village Tales Publishing. We intend to publish one anthology from this competition every year, for as long as the competition exists.

We've also hosted our 1st Annual Books, Cupcakes & Conversations event, Martha Juah Educational Foundation's premier literary event, celebrating progress in the literary and educational sectors of Liberia, while highlighting challenges, and discussing the way forward. We've held our Mentorship Meet-ups and Young Writers' Workshop, and also launched an online World Book Day campaign, aimed at igniting a passion for reading and storytelling amongst young Liberian girls and women.

Our ongoing projects include; the Annual Sexy Like A Book Poetry Competition for Liberian Girls, Sexy Like A Book's Enchanting Voices Anthology, Books, Cupcakes & Conversations, Sexy Like A Book's Mentorship Meet-Ups and Sexy Like A Book's Young Writers' Workshop; with several others to launch later this year.

Bringing young girls under our wings and sharing our path and experiences with them, is a wonderful blessing. We encourage you to join us to inspire them to dream big, and strive to achieve the unimaginable, in spite of societal and cultural limitations.

# Connect With Us

@sexylikeabook | @marthajuahfdn
Email: sexylikeabook@gmail.com
Attn: Ms. Patrice Juah

**visit our websites:**
www.marthajuah.org | www.patricejuah.com
www.sexylikeabook.com
www.liberialiterarysociety.org

༺⁂༻

## PLEASE SUPPORT OUR CAUSE
## MAKE A DONATION

Globally, many barriers continue to prevent girls from accessing quality education, as well as enrolling in, and completing secondary school. We believe that an improvement in the chances of the African girl having access to quality education, can only be achieved if we eliminate and break barriers such as female genital mutilation, child marriage, teenage pregnancy, poverty, violence against girls and women, the high cost of school etc., which continue to pose threats to, and prevent girls from accessing and completing primary and secondary school.

A 2016 UNESCO Institute for Statistics report states that girls are more likely than boys to never set foot in a classroom, despite all the efforts and progress made over the past two decades. According to UIS data, 15 million girls of primary school age will never get the chance to learn to read or write in primary school compared to about 10 million boys. Over half of these girls - 9 million - live in sub-Saharan Africa. In keeping with Goal 4 of the Sustainable Development Goals, which emphasizes the need to ensure inclusive and equitable quality education, and promote lifelong learning opportunities for all, Sexy Like A Book remains committed to combating the high rate of illiteracy in Liberia (52.4 %), through a holistic approach that engages girls, beyond the classrooms, harnessing their inborn talents, through mentorship, writing, public speaking, etiquette courses and community service etc. The overall goal is to equip them to meaningfully contribute to their communities and be active participants in decision-making on issues concerning their wellbeing.

We want to expand our reach to the 15 counties of Liberia, targeting girls (12-21 years old), particularly in the rural communities, through community outreach initiatives and awareness campaigns. If you've been touched by this book and the work we're doing, we encourage you to donate and join us as we nurture and develop Liberia's next generation of leaders.

All proceeds from this book will go towards scaling up and strengthening our current projects.

"Alone we can do so little; together we can do so much." ~ Helen Keller

# Patrice Juah

Editor

Patrice Juah is a Mandela Washington Fellow of President Obama's Young African Leaders Initiative (YALI), Writer, Poet, Entrepreneur, Broadcaster, Communications Strategist, Girls' Education Advocate, Global Speaker and former Miss Liberia, dedicated to changing Liberia's image within the international community. She strives to motivate and empower young women by supporting several local non-profit organizations' efforts in educating women on topics such as HIV/AIDs, teenage pregnancy, education, and workforce development. She is also the Founder and Creative Director of Moie, a diversified social enterprise with core competencies in media, public relations, events planning and retail management services.

As a published writer, she's currently the Girls' Empowerment Columnist for Vital Woman Magazine UK and blogs for Tropics Magazine's Tropics Voices Platform. Her writings have also been featured on PBS NewsHour, African Feminist Forum, Liberian Observer, Conversations on Liberia and the Sea Breeze Journal of Contemporary Liberian Writings. In 2013, she was invited by UNFPA to present her poem, "Fistula, I Have Conquered You", written to honor the survivors of Fistula at the 1st International Day to End Obstetric

Fistula. Patrice is the founder and chairperson of the Miss Education Africa Pageant, Africa's first Pan-African education pageant, which promotes and advocates for girls' education on the continent. She's also the founder and editor of "Sexy Like A Book", an academic initiative designed to inspire young women and girls to improve their perspective on reading, literacy and education. She's a regular contributor to the United Nations Mission in Liberia (UNMIL) radio show, 'Girl Power' that promotes self-esteem, confidence, and the importance of leadership in local communities.

Ms. Juah founded the Martha Juah Educational Foundation, named in honor of her mother, a retired primary school teacher of 47 years, to advocate for scholarships for young girls in rural Liberia. Patrice holds a bachelor's degree in Mass Communications and Political Science, an advanced certificate in Fashion Design, and a certificate in Business & Entrepreneurship. She was invited by former U.S. First Lady, Michelle Obama, in July 2014, for a roundtable discussion on Girls' Education in Africa, and served as an advisory committee member for the 5th Annual African Creative Economy Conference, held in Yaoundé, Cameroon, in 2015.

During the West African Ebola outbreak, she launched the "Ebola Is Not My Identity" campaign along with other artists to combat the problem of stigmatization. The goal of the campaign was to showcase creative works of art that reflected hope for Liberia on her path to recovery, other than the images of despair shown on the news wires at the time. In 2015, she was featured in Amina Magazine, as one of the new female faces of the African Creative Economy, and was also spotlighted by Brand Woman Africa in the same year as one of the women whose efforts are positively changing Africa one community at a time. This young, driven and vivacious woman believes that for Africa to succeed, Africans must make education a powerful driver and the strongest instrument in the reduction of poverty, improving health, gender equality, peace and stability. She's a member of UN Women's Civil Society Advisory Group on Liberia, sits on the board of the Liberia Literary Society, and recently served as keynote speaker at the 2016 Global Entrepreneurship Week in Geneva, Switzerland, as a guest of the U.S government. She describes herself as a "gem of unimaginable proportions".

*Patrice Juah*

www.ingramcontent.com/pod-product-compliance
Lightning Source LLC
Chambersburg PA
CBHW051815040426
42446CB00007B/676